OREGON

the Coloring Book

Featuring the artwork of *Jennifer Reynolds*

WESTWINDS
PRESS®

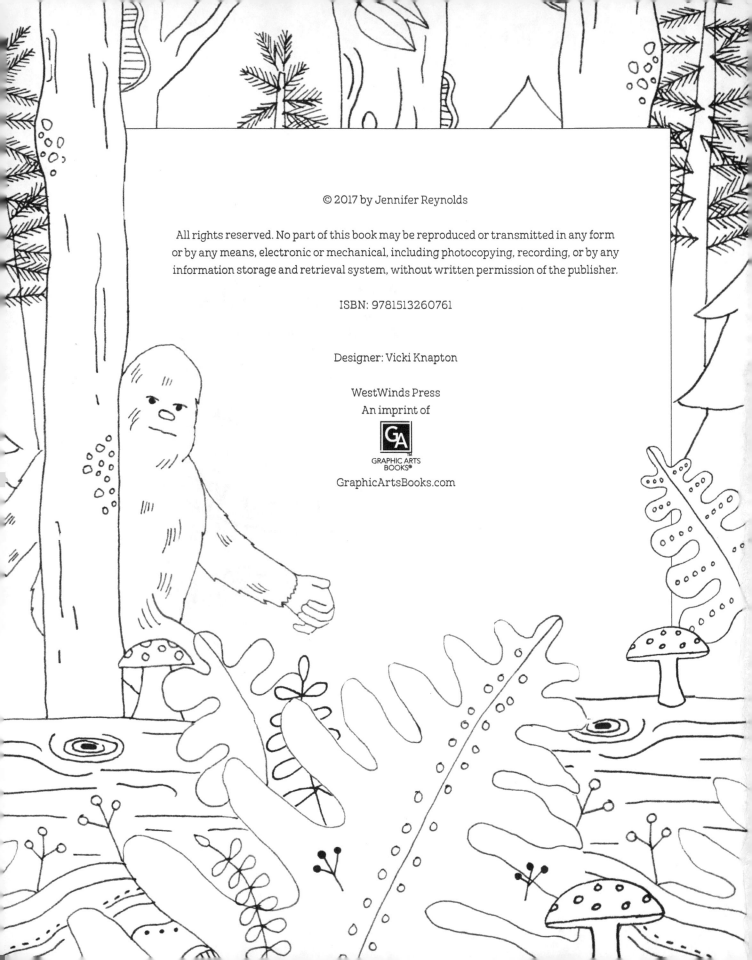

ISBN: 9781513260761

Designer: Vicki Knapton

WestWinds Press
An imprint of

GA
GRAPHIC ARTS
BOOKS®

GraphicArtsBooks.com

_____

This book belongs to

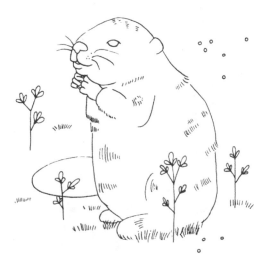

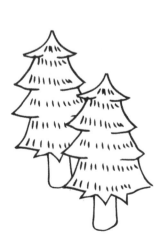

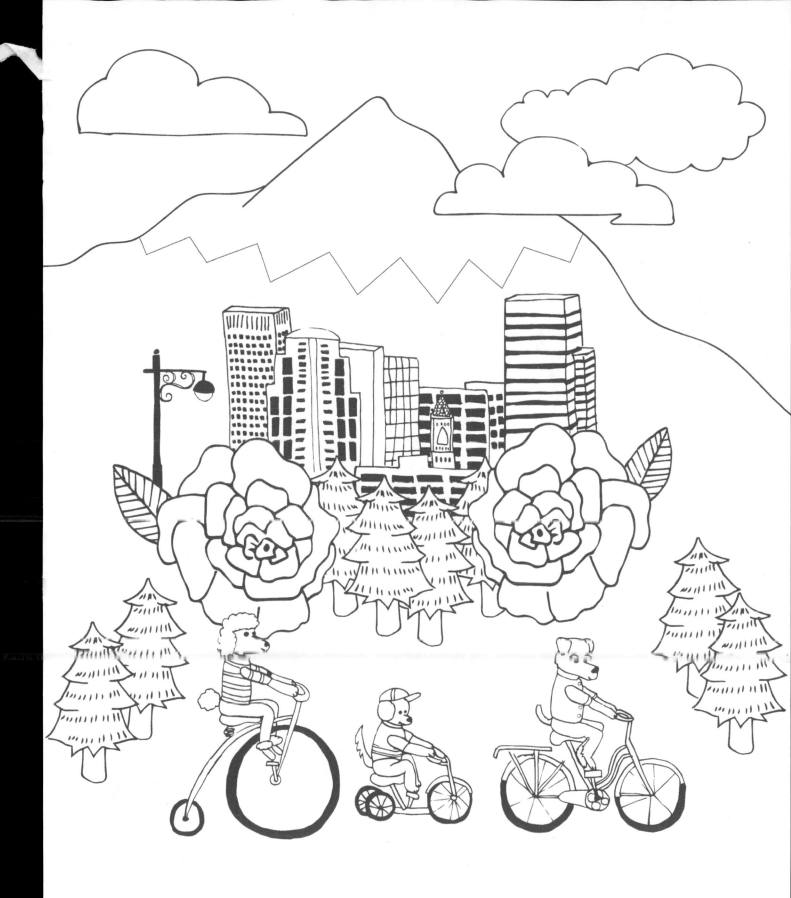

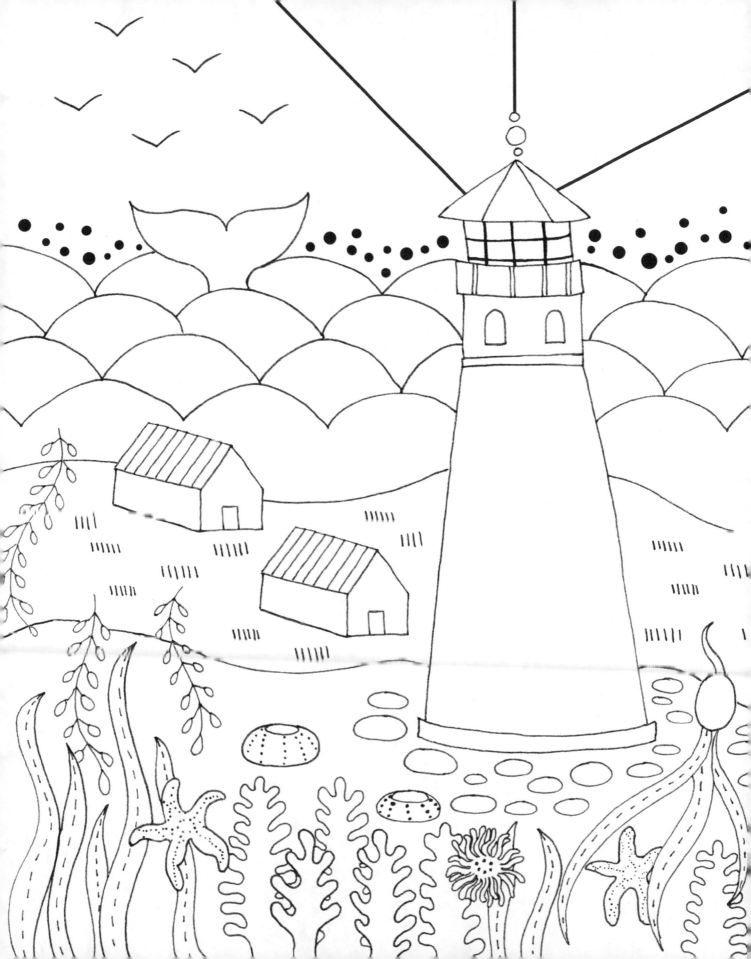

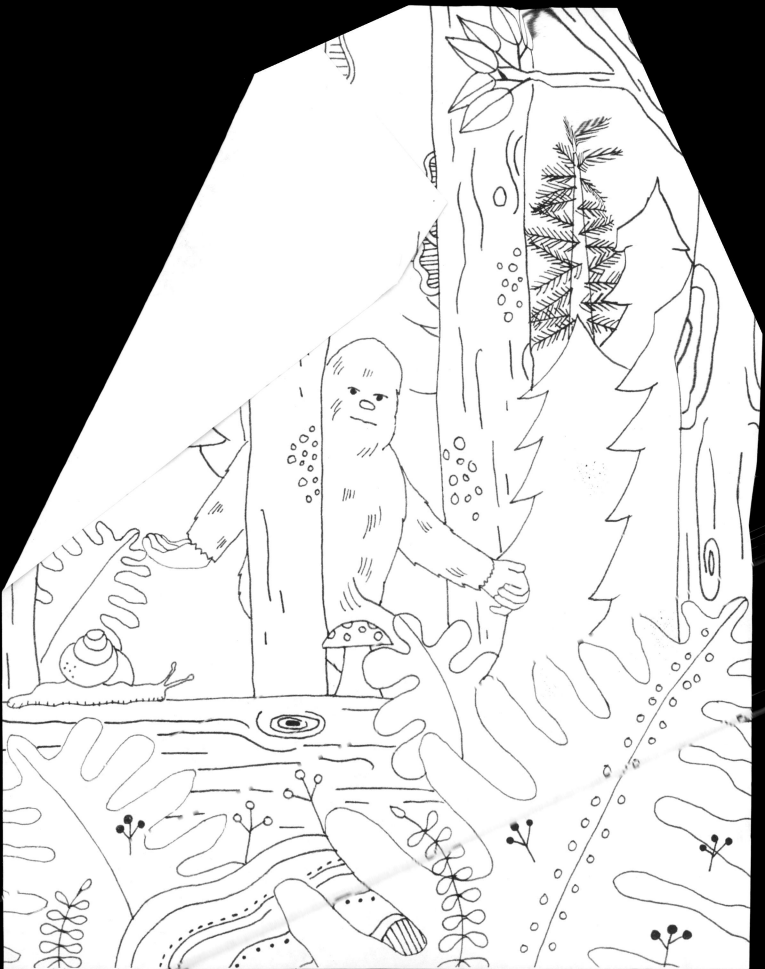

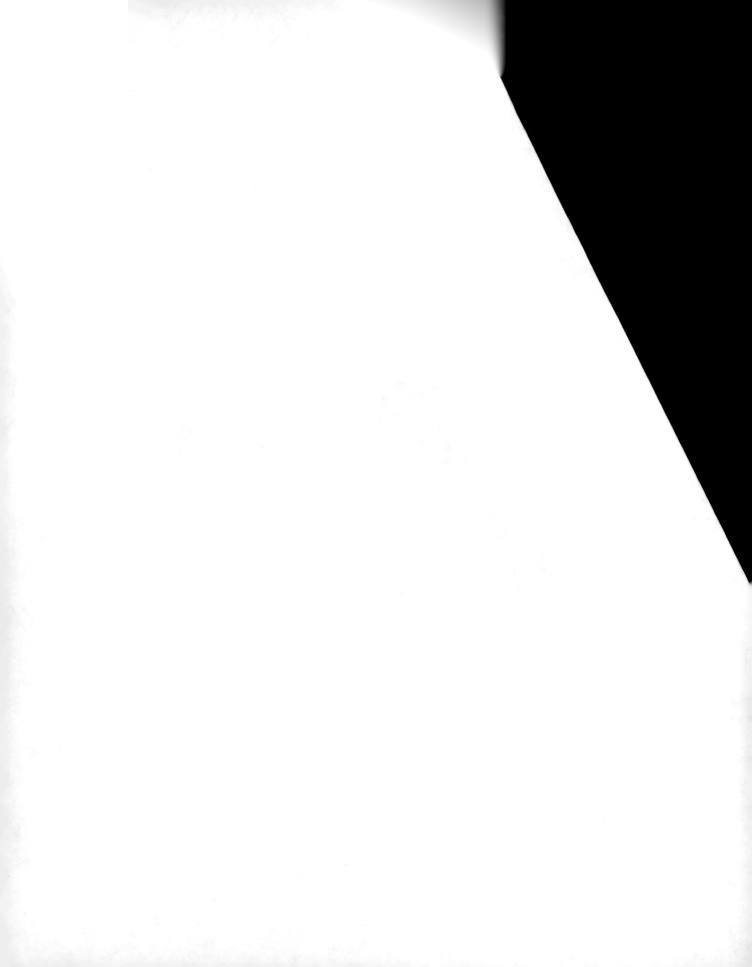

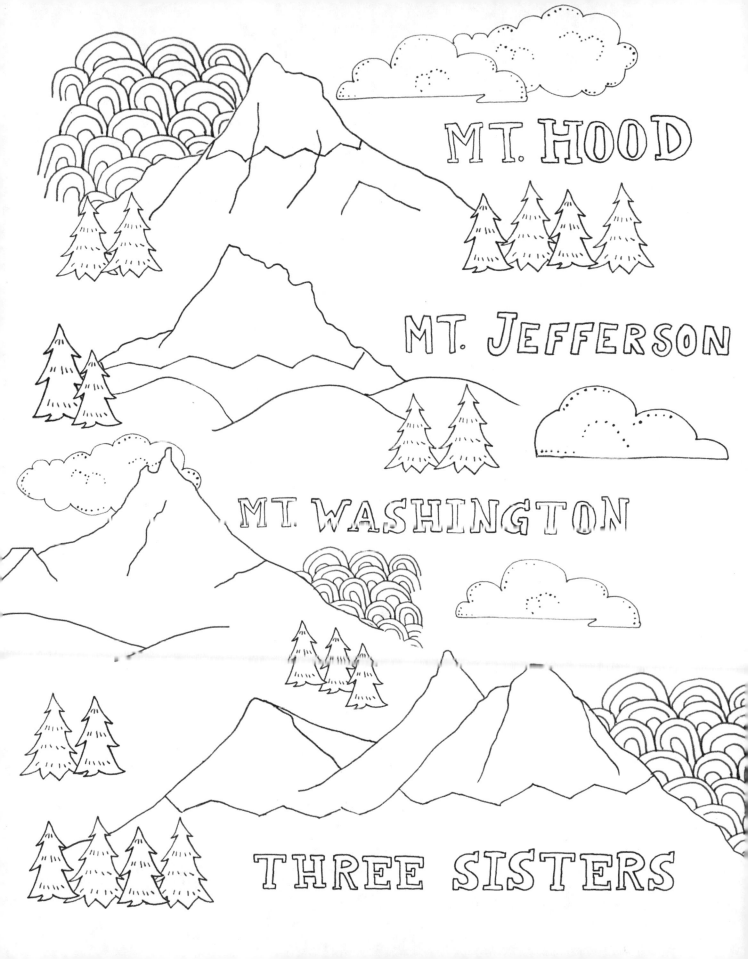

MT. HOOD

MT. JEFFERSON

MT. WASHINGTON

THREE SISTERS

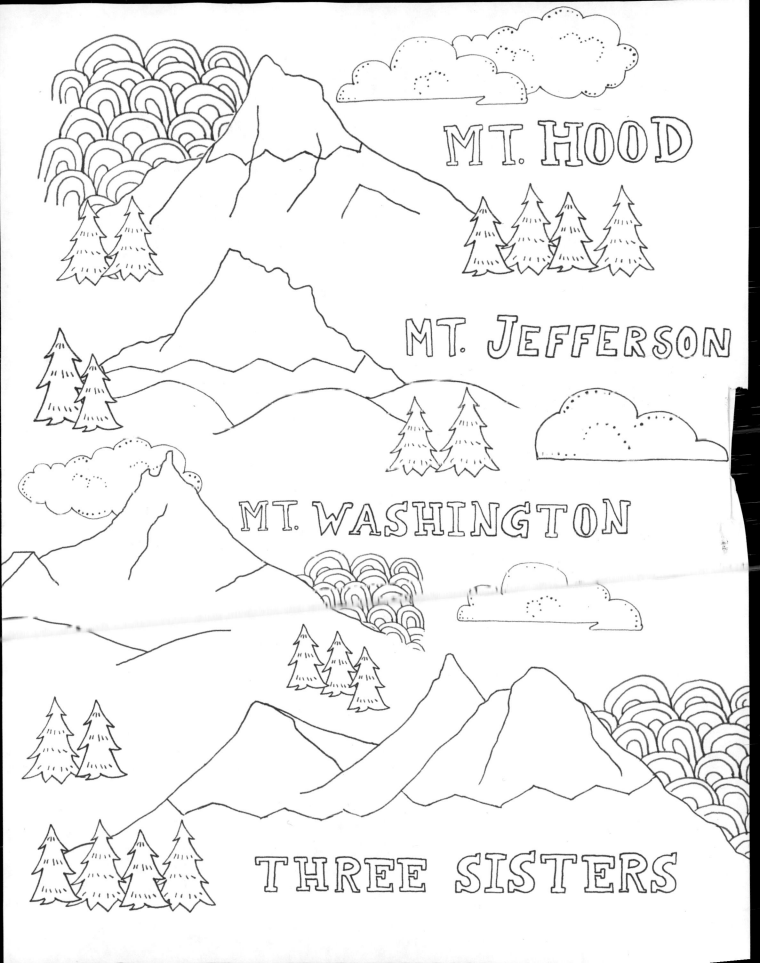

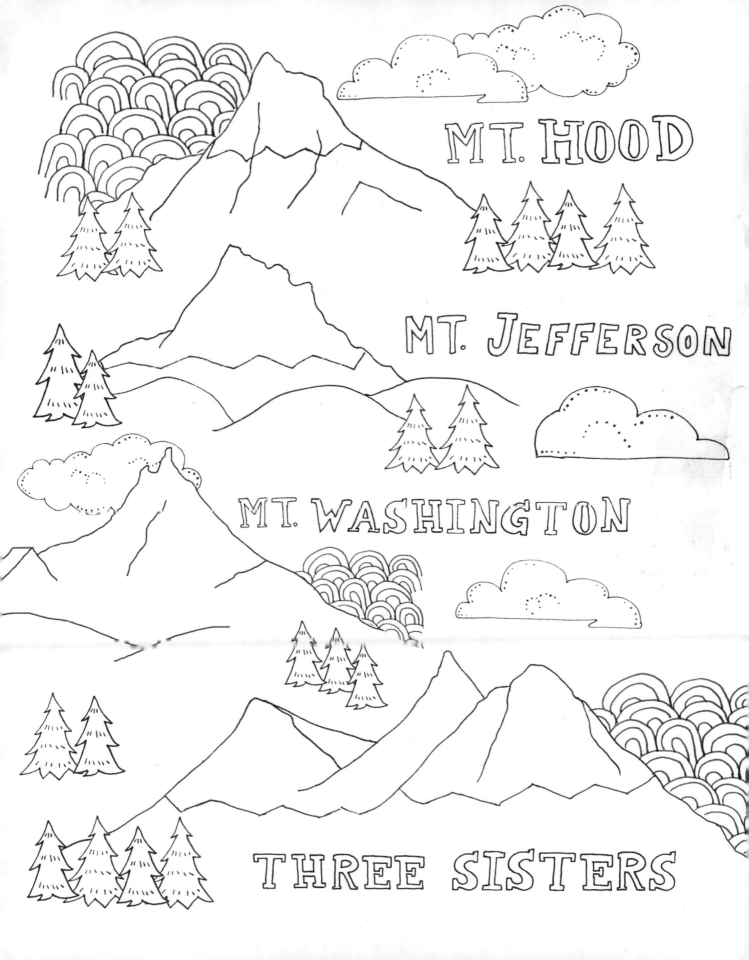

MT. HOOD

MT. JEFFERSON

MT. WASHINGTON

THREE SISTERS

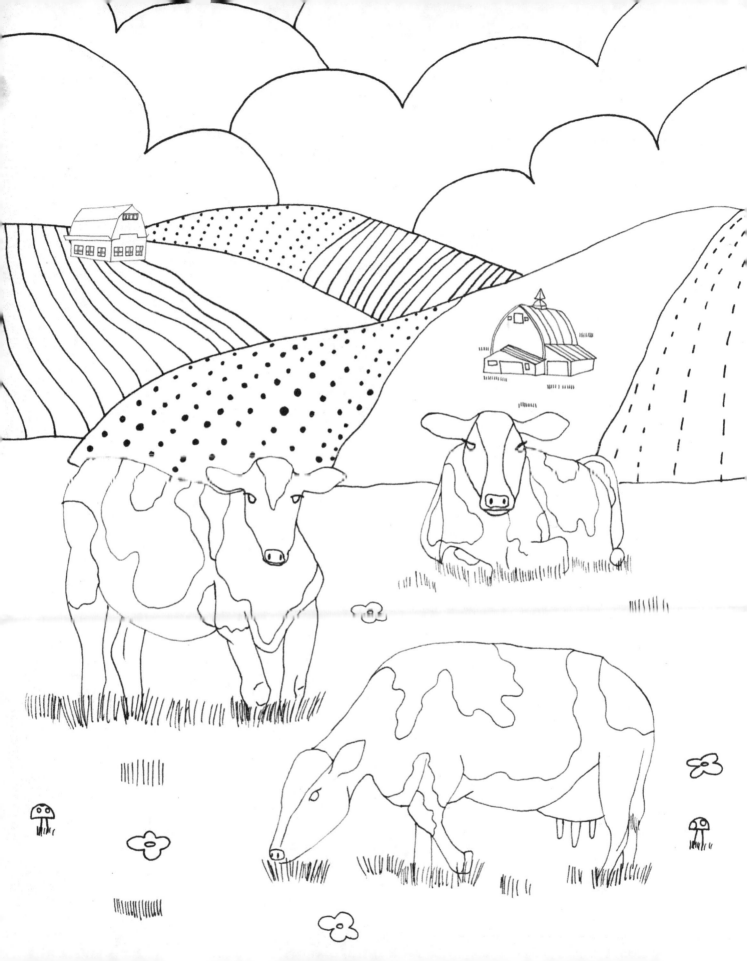

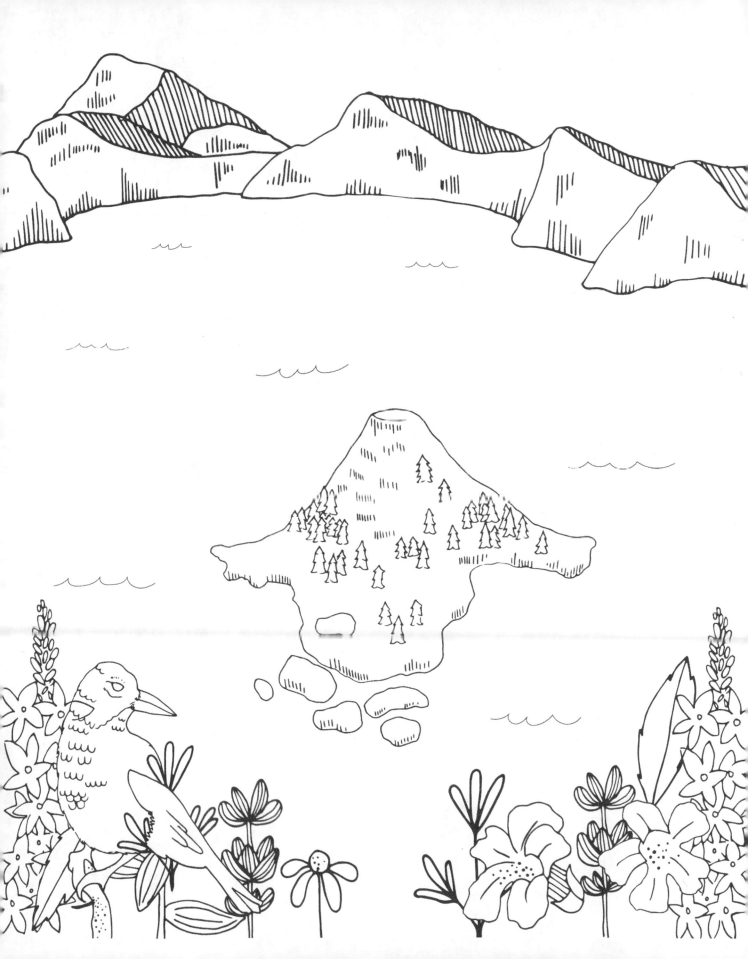

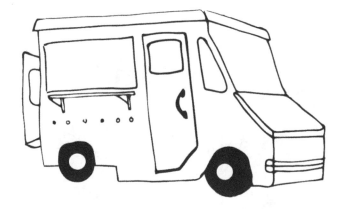

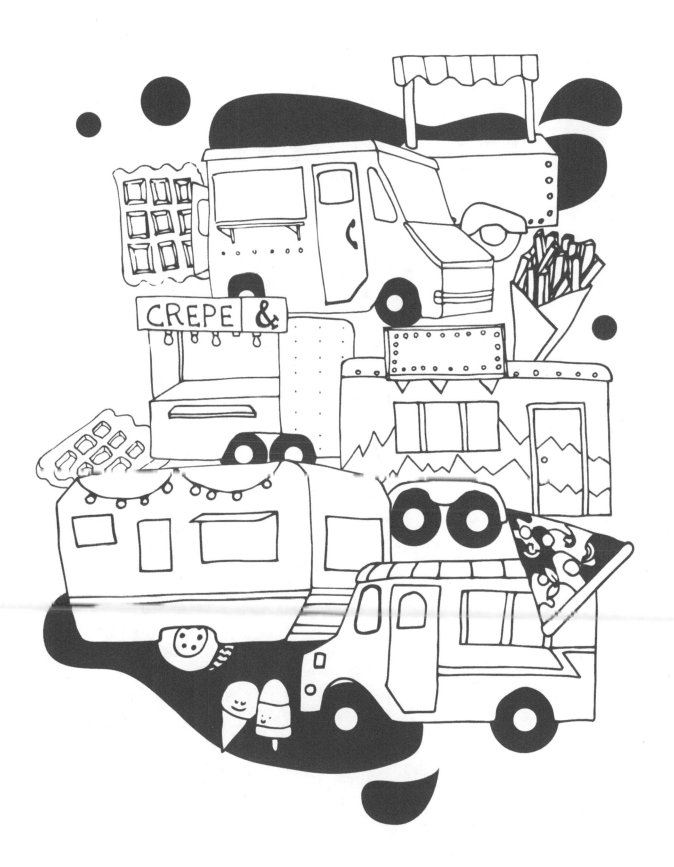

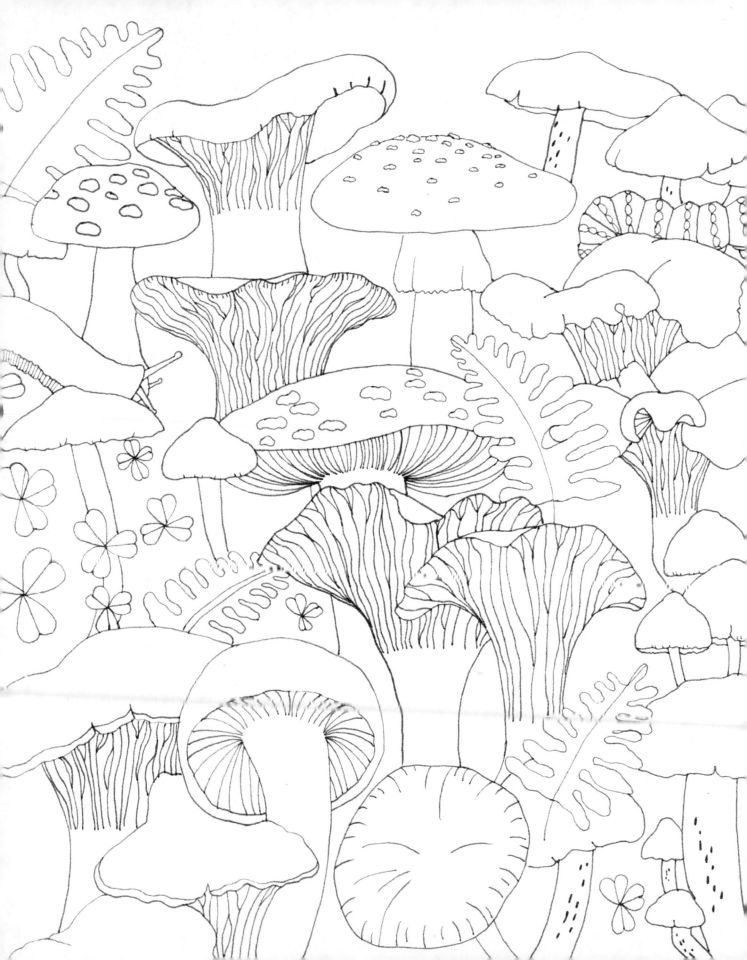

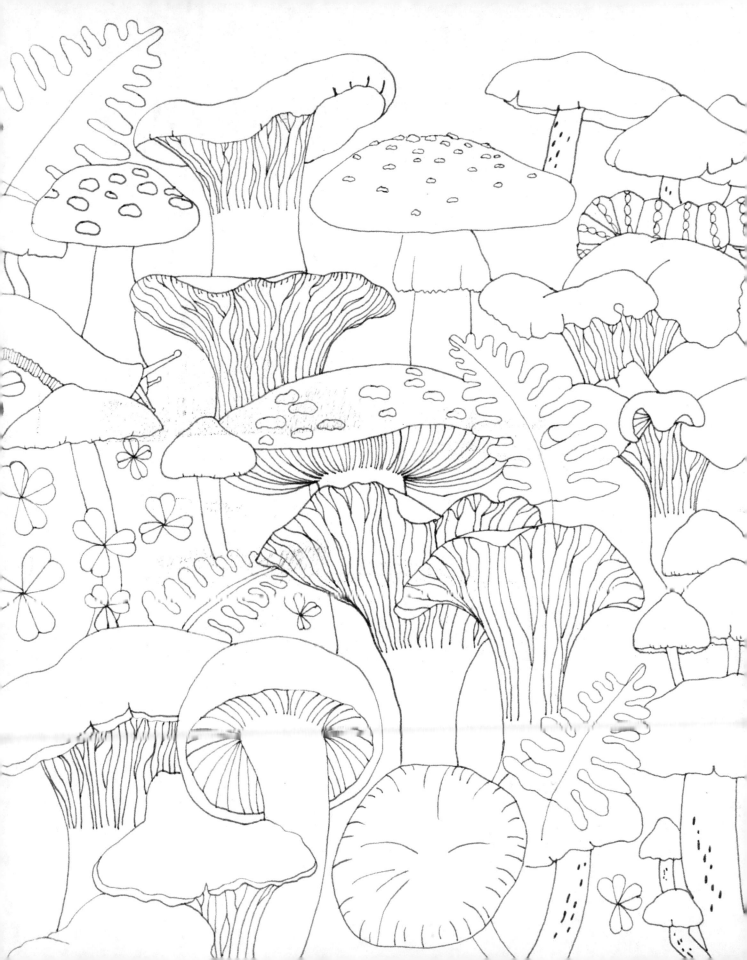

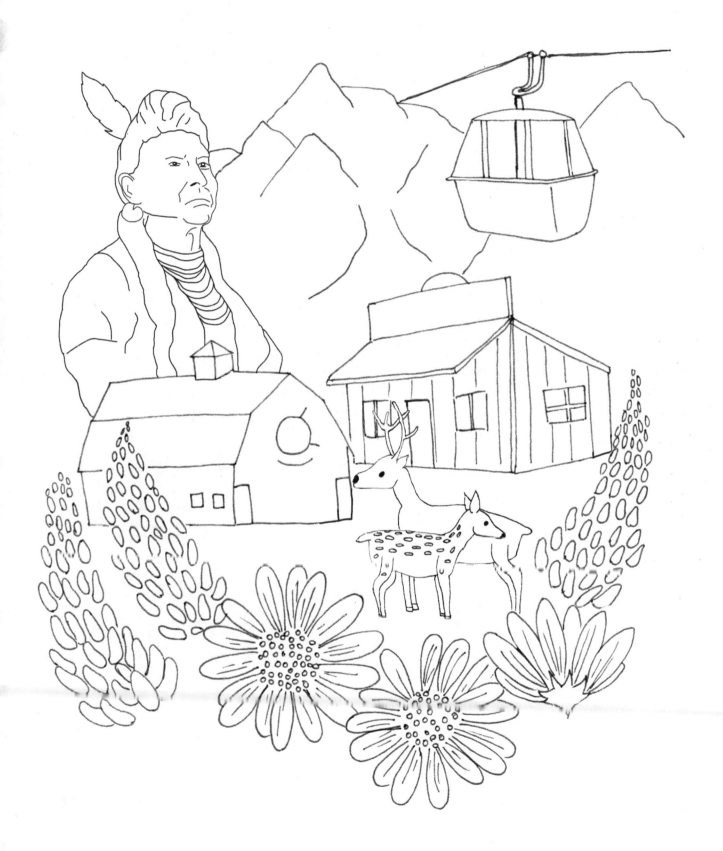

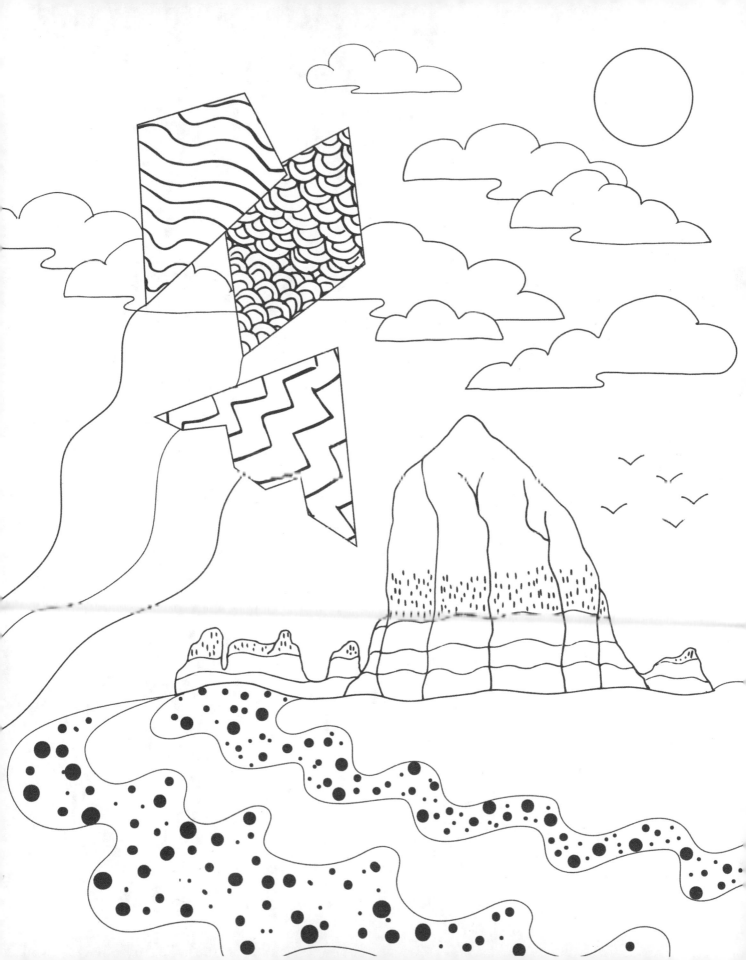

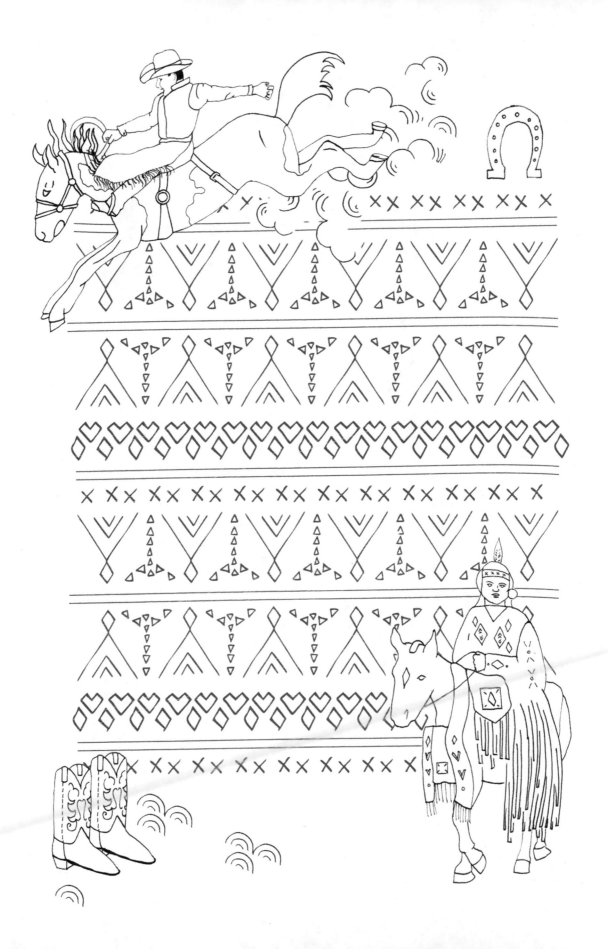

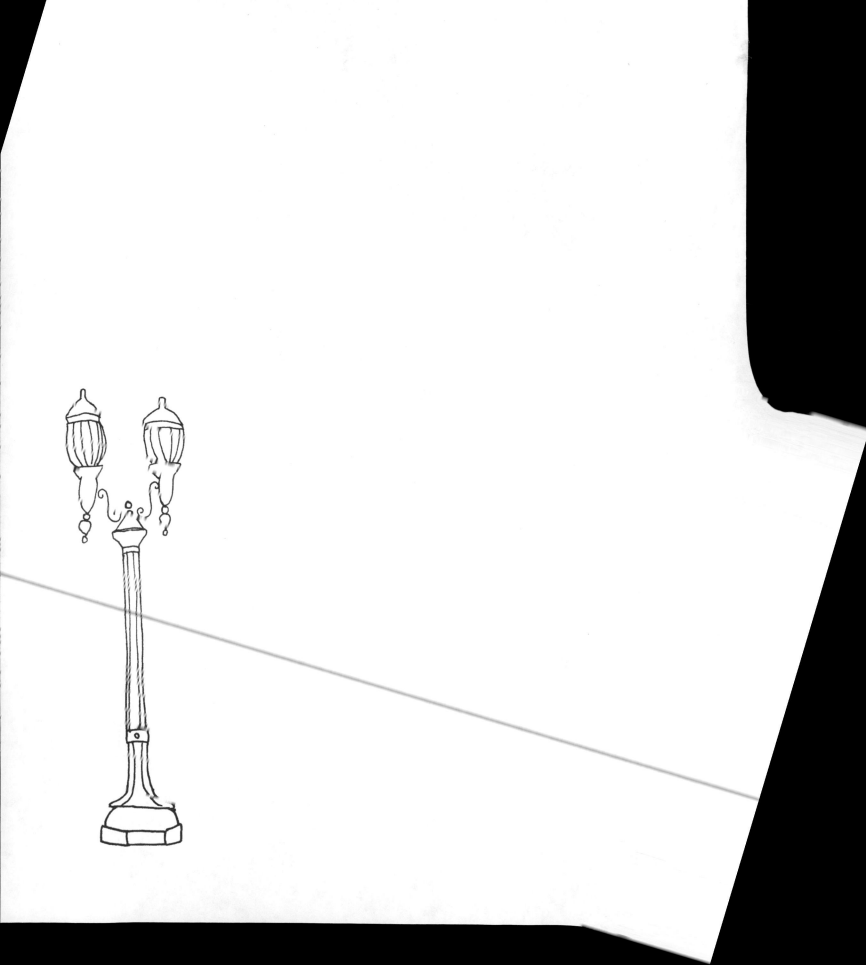

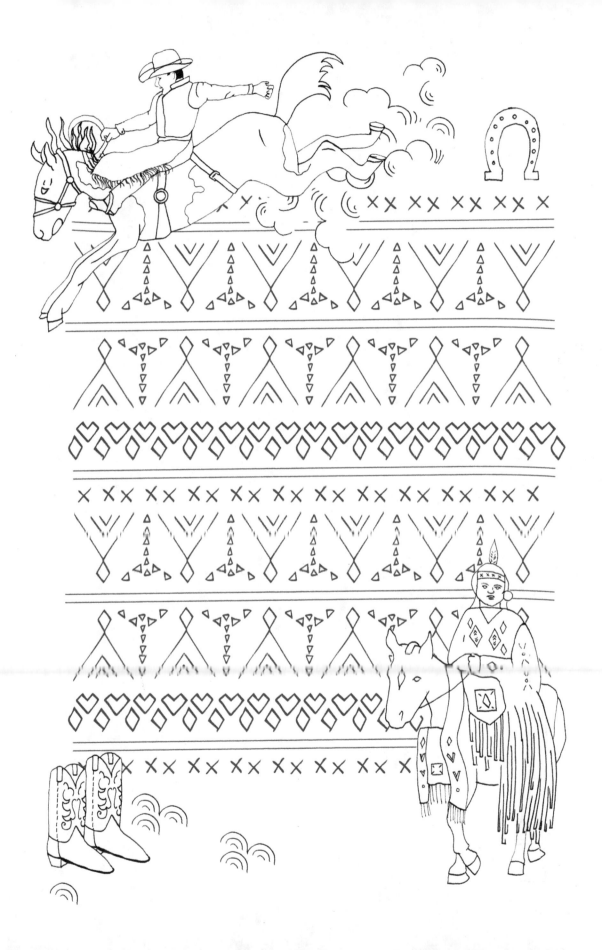

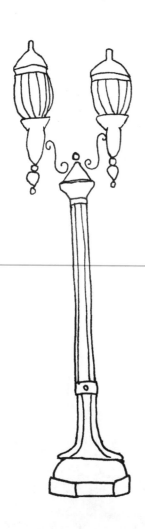

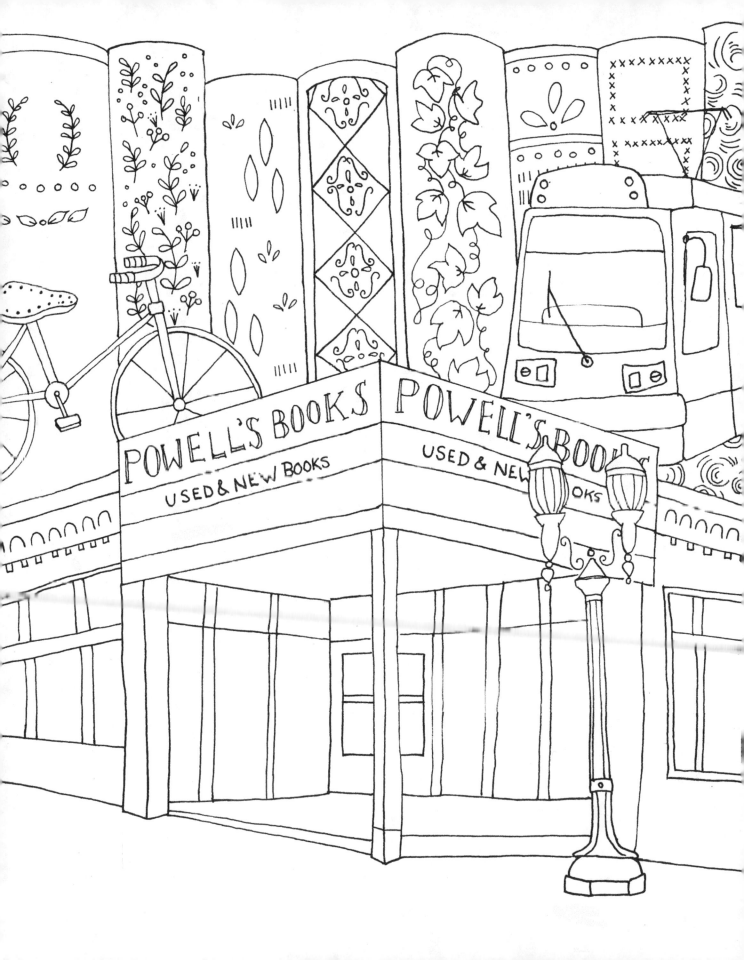

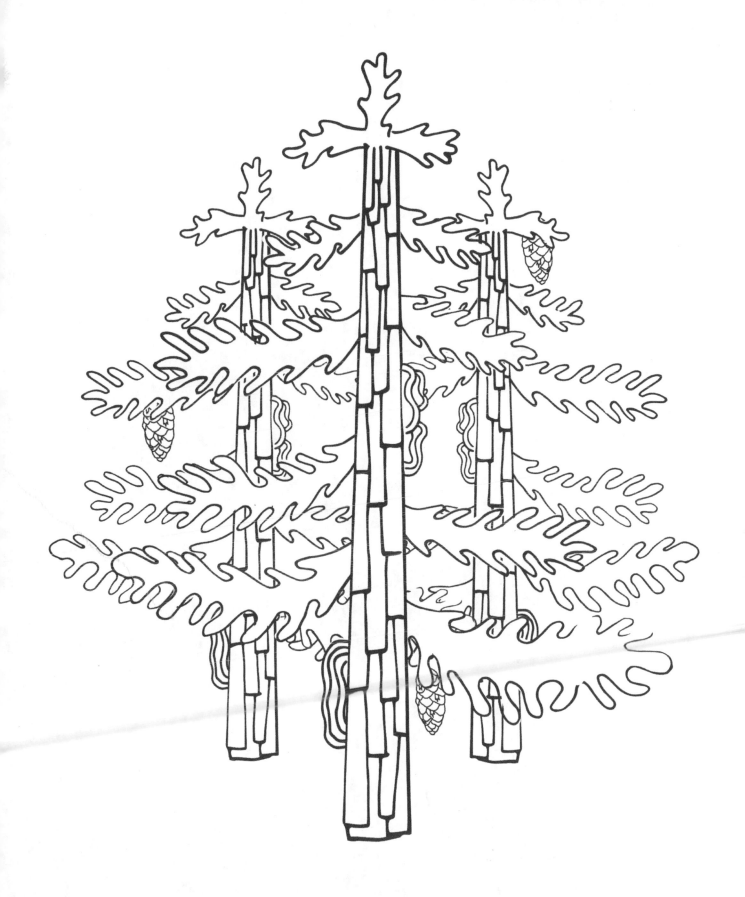

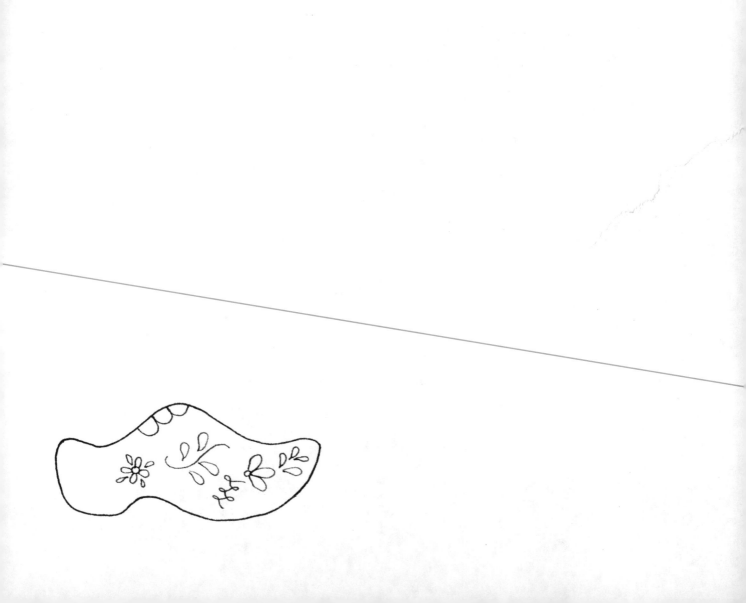

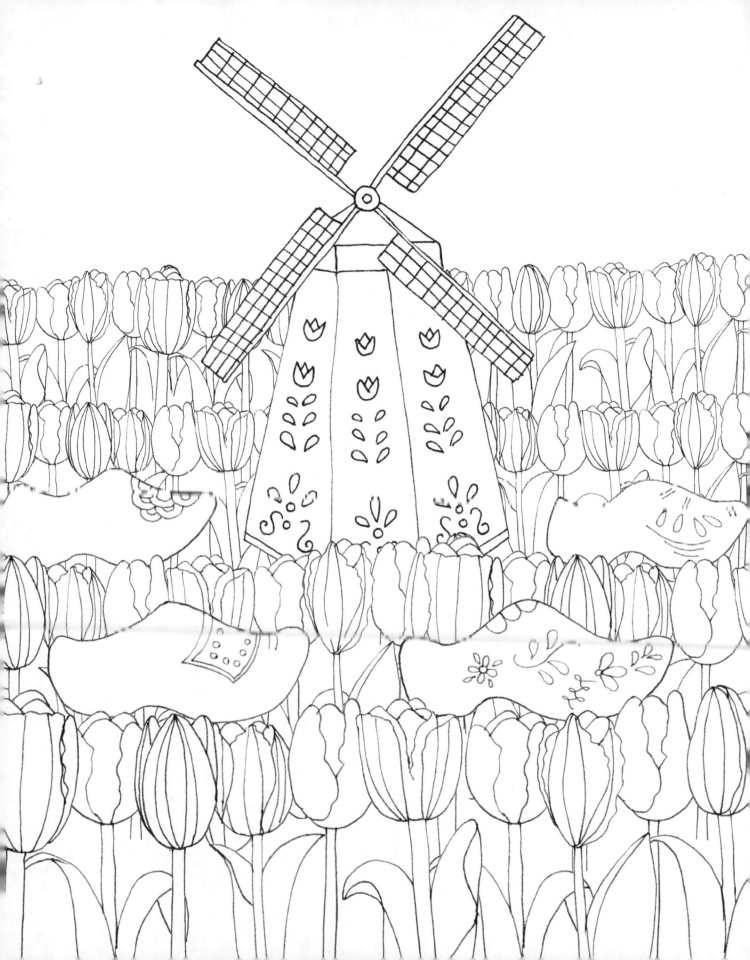

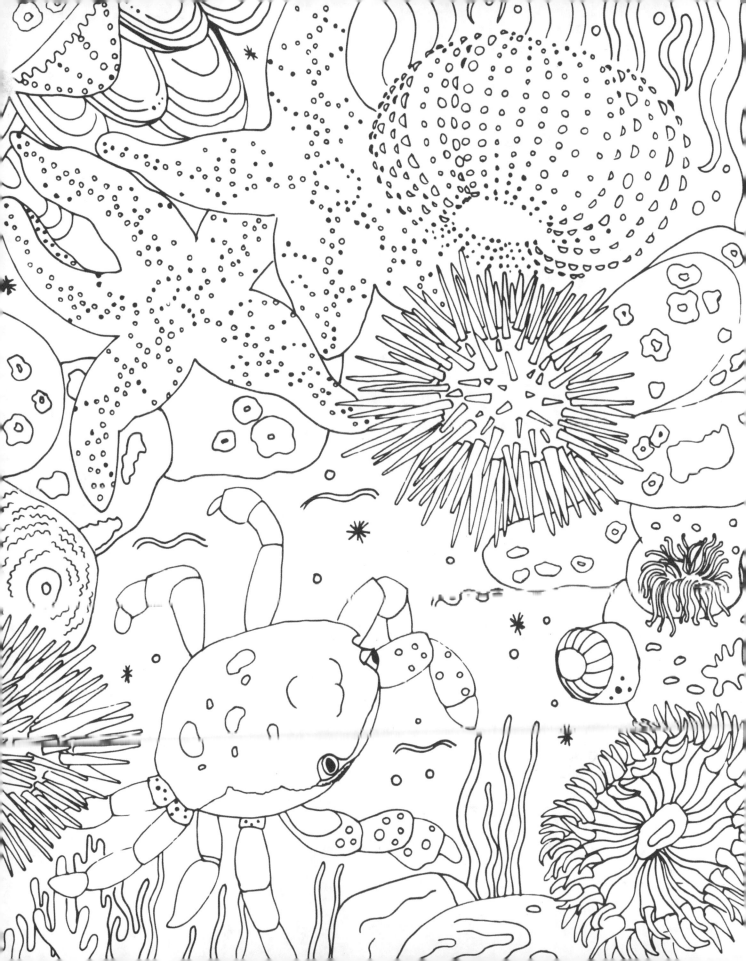

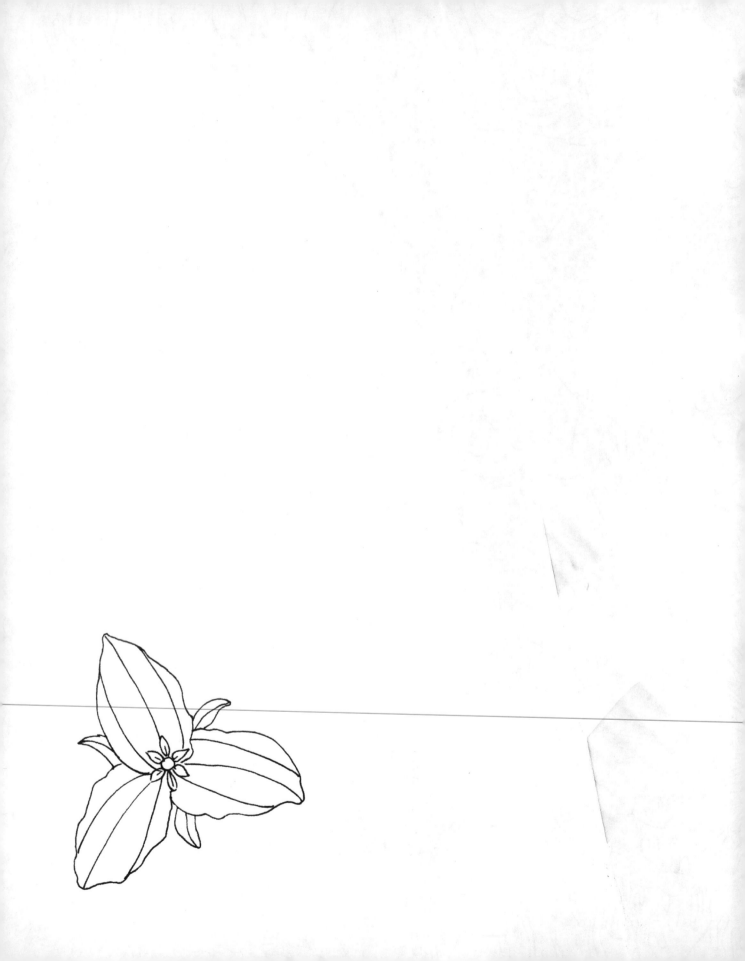

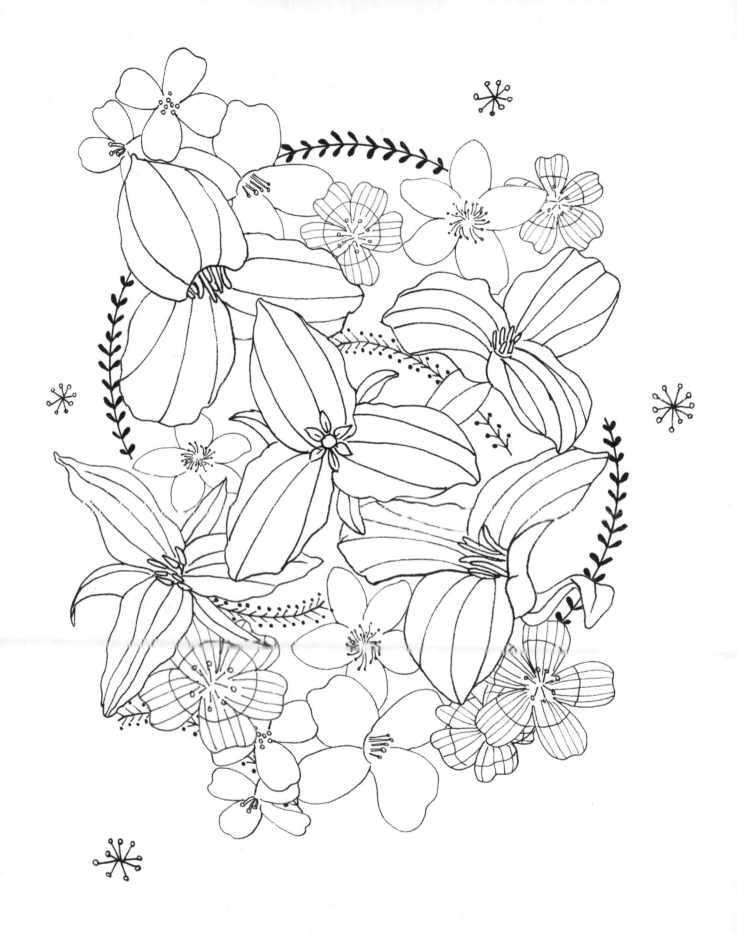

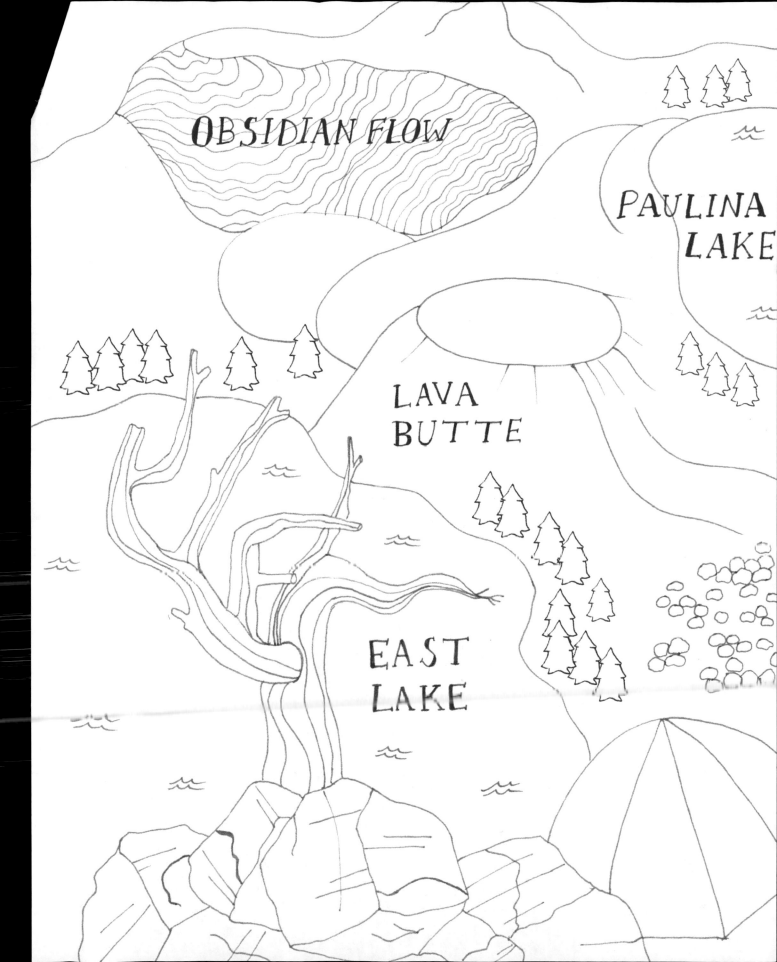

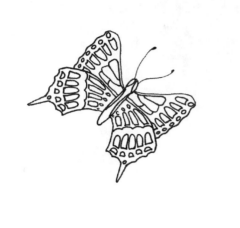

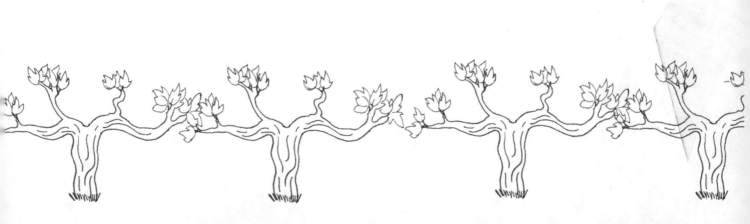

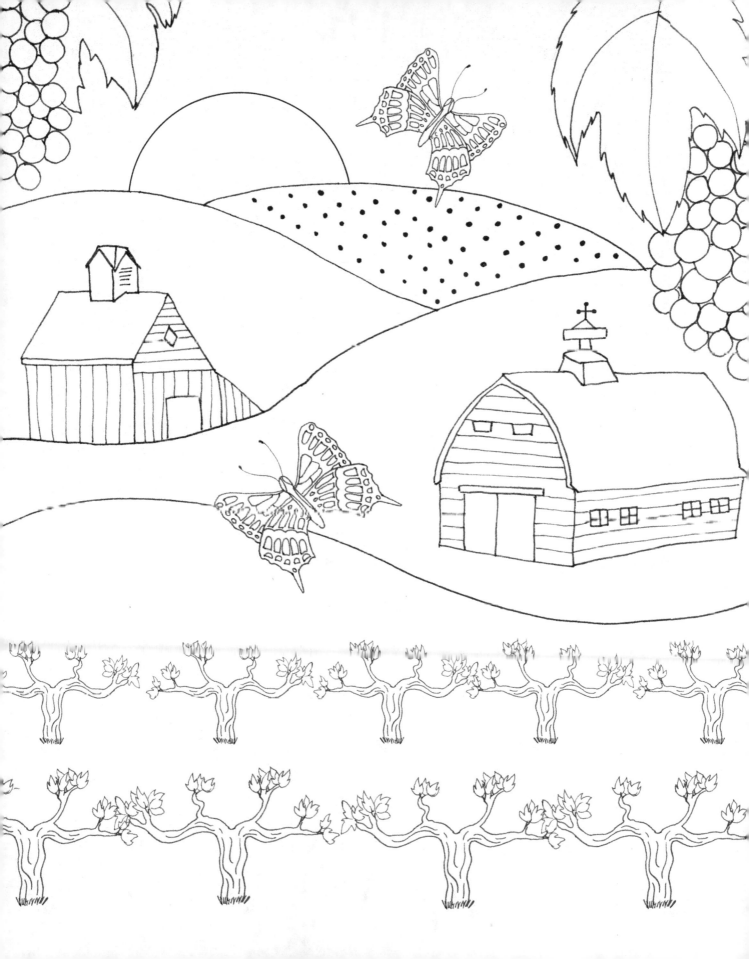

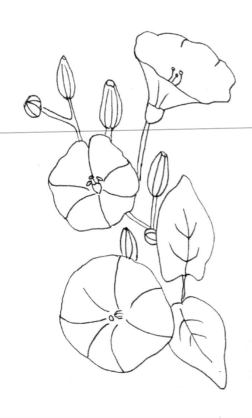

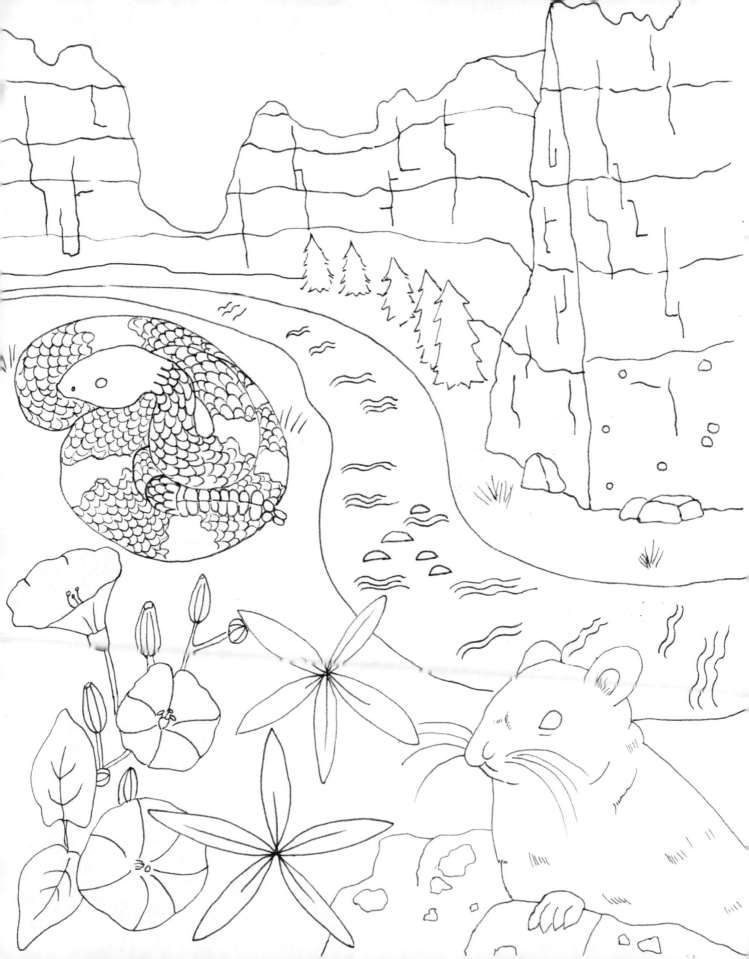

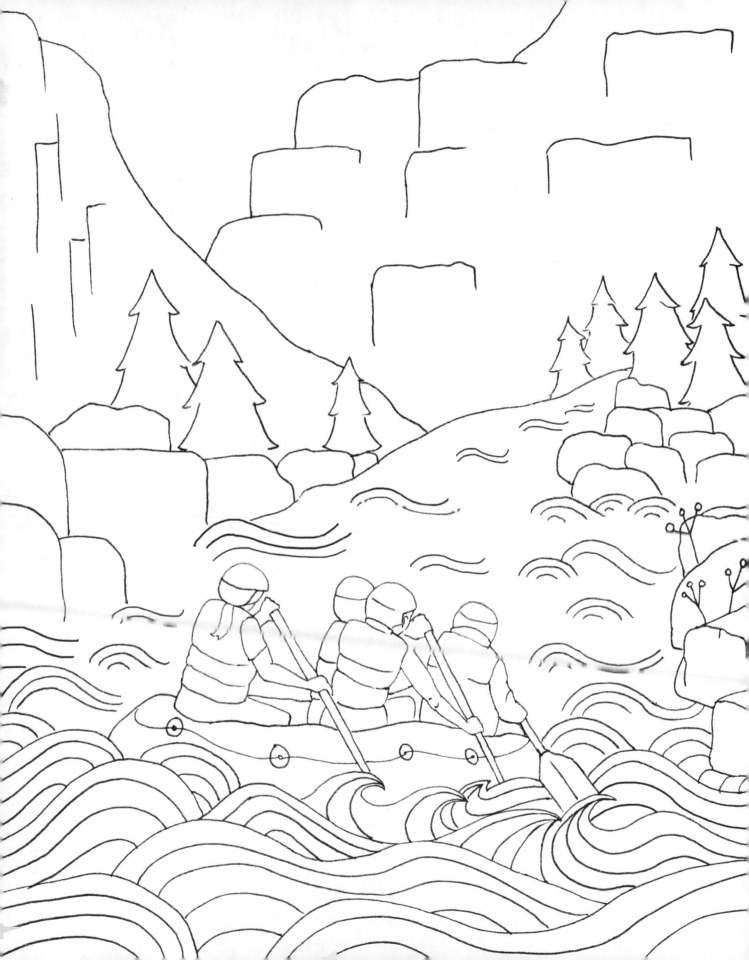

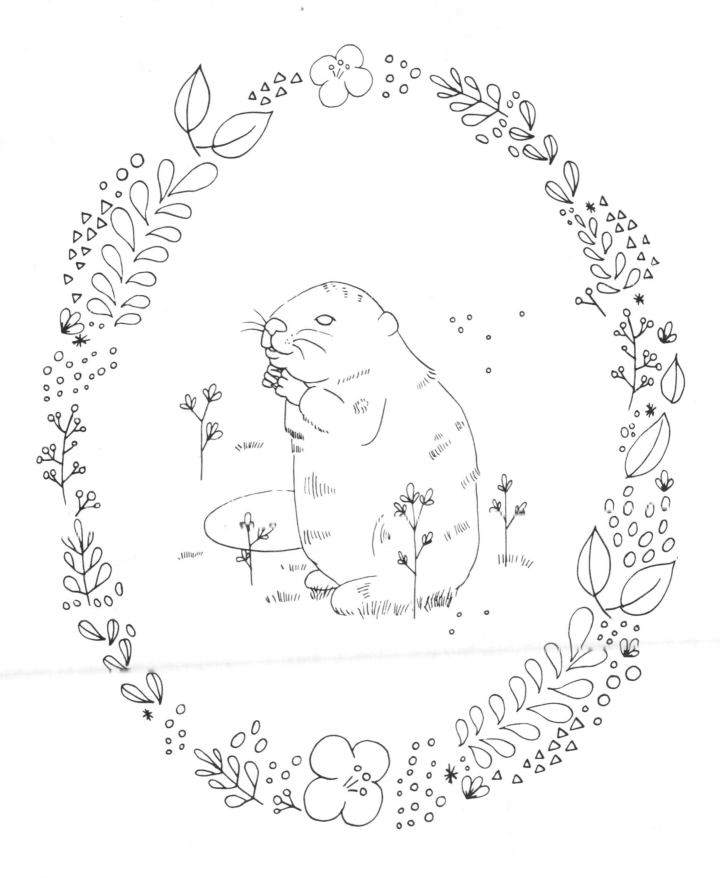

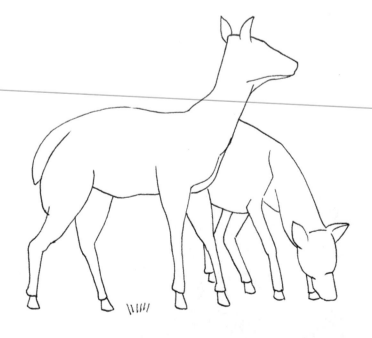

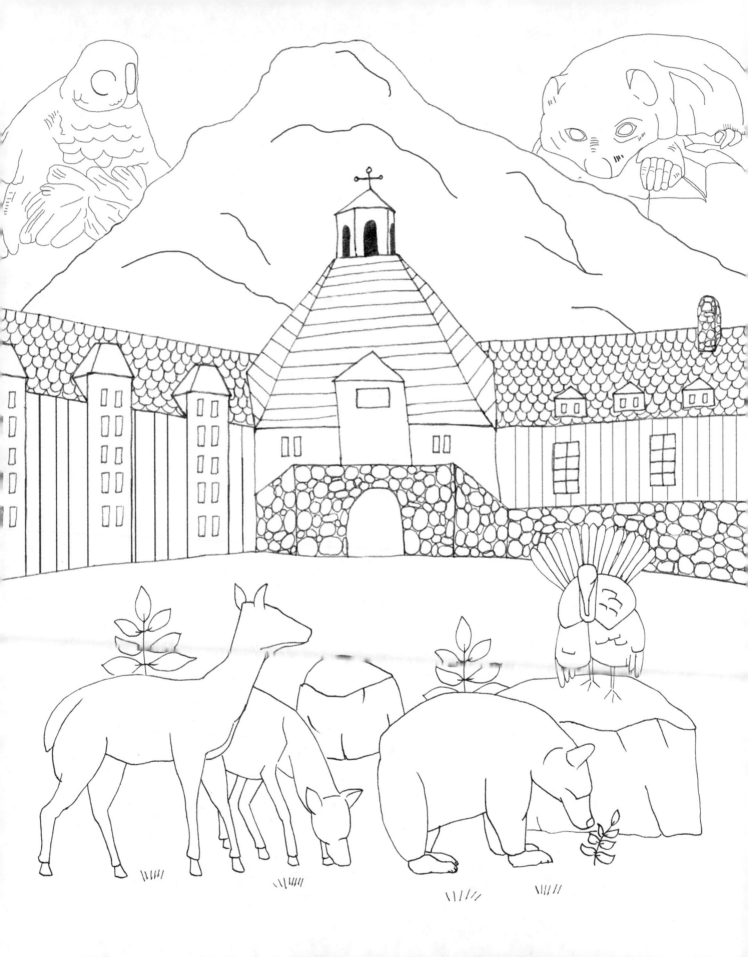

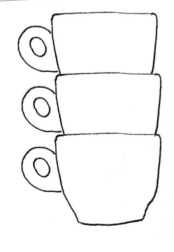

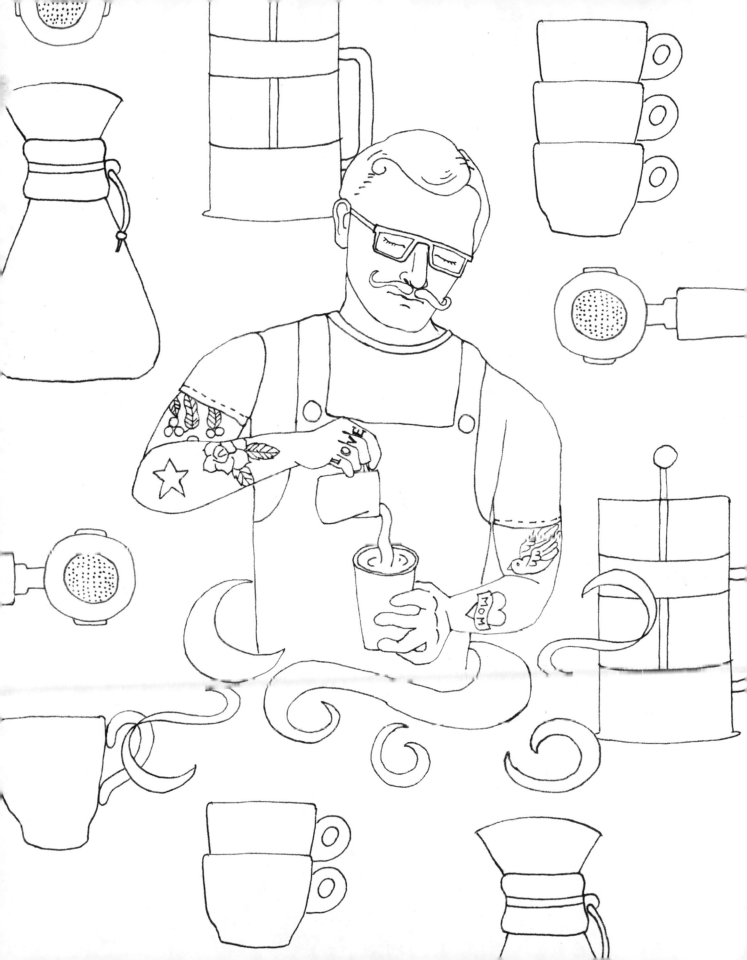

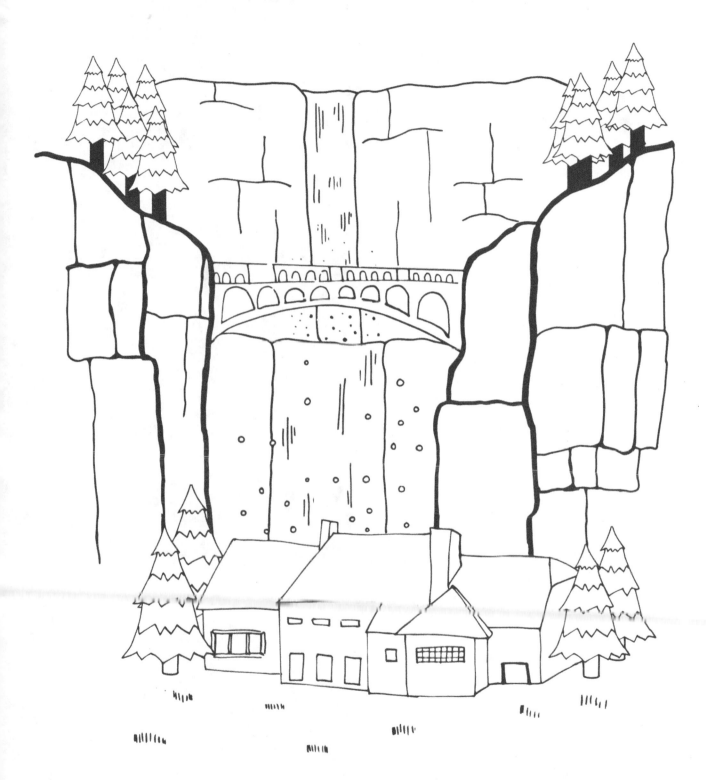